MASTERY
UNDER
PRESSURE

All that stands between
you and your goals... is YOU!

TINA GREENBAUM, LCSW
FOREWORD BY JEFFREY HAYZLETT

Book design by Camille J. Brown
Cover design by JB Lim

ISBN 978-1-7962-4121-1

Published by Kindle Direct Publishing (KDP)
www.tinagreenbaum.com

MASTERY UNDER PRESSURE

All that stands between you and your goals... is YOU!

Tina Greenbaum, LCSW

Foreword by Jeffrey Hayzlett

CONTENTS

Foreword

By Jeffrey Hayzlett

Primetime TV & Podcast Host, Speaker, Author and Part-Time Cowboy

Performing isn't just for actors. We all perform in multiple ways any given day—performing to reinvent ourselves in business, performing when we do keynotes or speaking engagements and performing in order to reach the goals and metrics that will increase our bottom line.

Business is constantly evolving and we need to adapt to all the changes taking place around us. One of my favorite adages is, "adapt, change or die." It couldn't be more apt to the world we live in, but the truth remains that not everyone is as nimble. For me, I'm able to pivot at a moment's notice and adapt to my surroundings with minimal disturbances. However, I also recognize that we're not all created the same in that regard. It's

OK not to be able to pivot quickly — it's not a competition, but you must pivot regardless.

Some people feel a disturbance in their 'force' when there are a lot of changes taking place around them. This is the part of the game where we need to stop and asses why we are so reluctant to change. What's holding us back? And how can we overcome it?

Sometimes we don't (or can't) identify what our obstacles are. We put ourselves in boxes, which become barriers and excuses that limit the stories we tell, resulting in complacency and inaction. And this is when we can get into trouble—inaction by paralysis. We must snap out of that paralysis. Borders should be like those between states: invisible. They should also be expandable, adaptable and permeable.

I call that steamrolling obstacles. We have all overcome obstacles to get where we are, but it is being able to use what we have learned to steamroll ongoing obstacles—those that prevent us from going to the next level. The only way to overcome these roadblocks is by putting them front and center – dealing with them head on.

I've seen many companies and individuals steamroll their obstacles by asking the right questions

and taking the right actions to disrupt convention-
al wisdom. You can, too!

Tina's book gives readers practical, tangible, and
actionable items that can help anyone willing to
take a leap of faith in order to elevate their lead-
ership skills. It'll teach you to focus on when to be
efficient and productive, and how to channel your
energy and transform it from negative self-talk
into productive thinking. The mind is a masterful
instrument, don't let it play you.

Acknowledgments

This book is the culmination of over three decades of integrating and synthesizing the teachings of my great mentors, as well as receiving incredible guidance, love, and support from my beloved family and friends.

Very specifically, Pandit Yogiraj Achala (Charles Bates) and Jason Shulman, my spiritual teachers, gave me the breadth and wealth of their knowledge, which has allowed me to find the wisdom that lives within me.

My business coaches, George Kao, Mark Hoover, Kane Minkus and Patrick Dahdal, great visionaries, in their own right, have encouraged me to seek my greatest potential by pushing the boundaries of my comfort zone and going after my biggest dreams.

My three sons, Andrew, Jesse and Scott Felluss have given my life purpose. Raising boys who are strong enough to be vulnerable, are mentally healthy and are positively influencing the next generation was my primary goal. They are exemplary young men.

My editor and great supporter, Scott Felluss has done double duty. Thank you, Scott, for your talent in helping me bring the world these teachings.

Their father, Elias Felluss, gave me the love of entrepreneurship and for that, I am forever grateful.

My parents, Mary and Mitchell Greenbaum were extremely wise and generous people. I am beholden to them for the foundation they gave me. Their common sense and humanistic philosophy have allowed me to give to my clients, my children and my world in a way that would not have been possible, had they not raised me in such a nurturing environment.

My brother and sister, Shirley Belitsky and Leonard Greenbaum have always encouraged me to reach my greatest heights.

To my sweet, loving, generous husband, Fred Sperber, I thank you for your patience, encouragement, and belief in me. You've made this chapter of my life special. My pursuit of reaching and teaching as many people as possible in the time I have left on this earth is a dream come true.

Introduction

Many years ago I was asked, "How old were you when you started helping people?" I honestly don't remember the age, but I do remember I was a very small child. It seemed to be the most natural thing to do: someone needed help and I could see a way to be of assistance. As I got older, I began to recognize that I had a gift for seeing solutions to problems that were not so obvious to my peers. When I couldn't see the path, I had an insatiable curiosity to find it. This trait has now been coined "emotional intelligence" and is defined as "the capacity to be aware of, control, to express one's emotions and handle interpersonal relationships judiciously and empathetically."[1] So, I had a great foundation to make my way through the world that helped me open seemingly impossible doors.

And yet my intuition was not enough: What I found

---

1 OED

was it could always be counted on as a great "hunch." There were many situations I would get myself into that required more than intuition.

I had a lot of dreams for myself: some of which were to be an expert speaker, a great dancer, a competent skier, and a competitive tennis player. I also moved around quite a bit in my adult life, which required starting my business as a therapist over more times than I would recommend. Needless to say, I had a knack for putting myself into high-pressure situations. In addition to reaching towards these lofty goals, I was hit with metastatic breast cancer while going through a nasty divorce. Trust me, I know pressure.

And so, life offered me a choice: I could succumb to the obstacles presented to me, or I could learn how first to manage and then to thrive in this challenging world. I chose the latter.

My strategy was to learn from the masters. What were the skills they possessed that I didn't? Spiritual teachers, business leaders, compelling speakers and great athletes were my role models—all champions in their own right.

What I'm presenting to you in this book is a touch of their wisdom through the prism of my own experiences.

How to Get the Most From this Book

Why I Wrote this Book

This book is a compilation of a lifetime's worth of information, training and experience. It's likely that you may skim the contents and say, " I know this stuff." The topics are now in the mainstream media and it is common knowledge that stress can be debilitating. However, *common knowledge* is not necessarily *common practice*.

Over the years, I would listen to clients share their insights about their families of origin in order to possibly identify why they thought and behaved as they did. This information, as interesting as it might have been, did not solve the problem of what to do and how to achieve the success they so desired—especially in the moments when quick thinking and acting were required. Knowing how to quiet the body so the mind can make good decisions is the crux of this book.

How to Read this Book

This book is filled with exercises which will help you accomplish the goal of managing your stress and creating peak performances. They go hand in hand.

You can read through this book to grasp the big picture of where we're going then come back and do the exercises, or you can follow each page as you would a workbook and practice each exercise as you go along.

The most important factor to remember is that we are creating new neural pathways through practice and repetition. You will get the best results if you approach the methods presented here as you would any new skill that you want to master. Simply reading and understanding the material will not get you to mastery.

However you read, I recommend that you keep a journal while you progress through this book both for tracking your individual progress and for processing each chapter and exercise in the moment.

You are also invited to join our Facebook Community: *Mastery Under Pressure Community.* Here, you can post questions and get support from the community. I am active on this page and will respond in a timely fashion.

If you are interested in understanding where you are personally before beginning any exercises in this book, feel free to take my online Assessment Quiz at **www.masteryunderpressure.net**.

Here's What to Expect from Reading this Book

Change is the only thing that we can count on in this life. If you are flexible and can "ride the waves" of change, your life will be more enjoyable and meaningful. Learning how to live on your edge of discomfort is the path to growth and transformation. If you ask nothing of yourself, your life will become stagnant. If you ask too much of yourself at one time, you will overwhelm your nervous system and sabotage your progress. But, if you follow the progression of the exercises in this book with a commitment to practice, you can expect to feel calmer, clearer, and excited about taking on new challenges with confidence.

Here's to your success!

CHAPTER 1
On the Job Training

In 1983, I got my first job as a psychotherapist at the Washington Hospital Center in Washington, D.C. on one of the first eating disorder units in the United States. At that time, the term bulimia had only been in existence for fifteen years. There was little precedent for treating anorexics or bulimics. Making good decisions under the pressure that patients were experiencing at the time was clearly the problem to be solved.

As a matter of fact, I was given a manual for treating alcoholism, with "alcoholism" crossed out and "eating disorder" put in its place. I was really on the ground floor and these young women were to be my greatest teachers.

I quickly noticed that my traditional Western "talk therapy" model did little to help them. We would delve into their histories and their behaviors but to little avail. The first talk that I ever gave was entitled, "The Intelligent, Insightful, Creative, But No Change Bulimic."

Once a week, we would take the patients to the hospital cafeteria so they could begin to face the challenge of making food choices on their own. You might have thought they were on the precipice of a cliff on the Coastal Highway. This was a high-pressure situation.

I watched them carefully and noticed their body language and the way they talked to themselves and really began to appreciate the level of complexity they were dealing with. Making a good decision under pressure was clearly the problem to be solved. I didn't know yet what to do, but I intuitively knew that their minds and the bodies had to be aligned. I had to get underneath the mind chatter into the unconscious – the place where real change had to take place. There was no way they could succeed while being so anxious and talking to themselves with such disdain.

The solution to success here was truly a mystery. I became obsessed with how to help these patients.

My first insight came while taking my first yoga class. During the last posture at the end of class,

Shivasana (or the corpse pose), we lied down and were guided into a deep state of relaxation, allowing our muscles and mind to relax after doing the more exertive postures. This was the first time in my life I ever felt so relaxed; my mind was clear, quiet, unencumbered from fear, concern or emotion. This experience got me even more obsessed with finding a solution for helping my eating disorder patients.

I remember saying to myself, "Wow! There's a whole world out there concerning the alignment of mind and body." I thought if I could understand what was scientifically happening to me in this state, I could really help my clients to let go of the past, to be in the present, to have a sense of inner calm and laser-like focus. Perhaps then these patients could make good decisions under pressure.

This inquiry led me to all sorts of trainings and workshops, teachers, mentors, gurus, while at the same time working with a myriad of clients – many of whom were business professionals, athletes, dancers, performers and anyone else who was to or wanted to be able to perform at an optimal level under pressure.

I began combining all sorts of these disciplinary

wisdoms with modern science. Working in concert with the universal laws of nature, I found I could more quickly help my clients make good decisions under pressure: To my delight, my eating disordered clients were recovering from their incredibly stubborn disorders and other clients I tried this method with were improving dramatically, too.

Back then this practice was called the "path of mysticism." Indeed, back then skeptics said, "don't let anyone know what you are doing—it's too woo woo." Now, however, science is proving many of the miracles we once attributed to mysticism. "Neurological re-patterning," "energy psychology," "mindfulness," and "conscious re-programming" are some of the terms we currently use. With the discovery of brain imaging we now know there are pathways to managing anxiety, to dealing with trauma, and to making good decisions under pressure.

Many people think we can "get rid of" old habits. We don't get rid of anything. We just interrupt the old patterns and create new patterns and pathways, which greatly expand our capabilities. With an unstoppable mindset, we are no longer on automatic pilot.

If you just locate the patterns and triggers in both your mind and your body, you begin to see yourself from a space of new awareness. Rather than being a victim of your history—that place where your body responds before you even have a chance to make a choice—you learn to slow down the mind and insert thought in the space between the stimulus and the response. Here, you are making the unconscious *conscious*: responding instead of reacting. I understand after many years of experience that this interruption is very difficult to achieve without a guide because the unconscious, by its nature, is unconscious.

When you know how to initiate the relaxation response and recode your patterning, you can make better decisions under pressure. You can achieve more than you ever expected and begin to enjoy the process more. If you're a business professional you get to deliver presentations, raise capital, and impress your superiors to get the raise, to get the promotion, and to get the opportunities. If you are an athlete you get to readjust quickly if the outcome is not headed in your favor, to pull from behind, to win more championships. If you're a performer, you get to be masterful at your art with a sense of inner calm and confidence.

Having tested these strategies and techniques on

thousands of clients over the years and having raised three of my own high performing children through the filter of these techniques, I have been frequently referred to as the "High-Performance Mom." I can be very sweet and nurturing, but I can also help you whip your mind into shape.

CHAPTER 2
Case Study

Before she met me, Samantha came to the United States from France to work in the hospitality industry. Her parents had owned a small restaurant and she had a good deal of knowledge and expertise in running an eating establishment. However, she wasn't quite prepared for the intensity and pressure that was evident in the kitchen of a temperamental chef in a five-star Manhattan restaurant. In a very short period of time, her confidence was shattered and she started questioning the wisdom behind her career choice.

At the same time, Samantha was endowed with a great deal of emotional intelligence and business acumen. She gravitated towards Management. She really enjoyed team building and guiding her staff. This was the point at which she realized she needed help and sought my services.

We began by assessing what was working for her and what was not. She clearly saw her "people skills" as her greatest asset but was struggling to cope with what she saw as unreasonable demands from her superiors. She felt if she could manage the pressure in a creative way, she could regain her confidence and excel in her industry.

I always say that mental toughness is not a natural sport; it's a learned sport. Samantha had all the right ingredients to become successful but lacked the skills and training to help her shine in the process.

To achieve her desired success, Samantha and I went through mental and mindfulness training, starting with the topic of **focus**. She was able to identify the elements in her work that, if she paid attention to them, would constitute a job well-done. Emphasis on these focal elements was a big shift from her absorbing the tension that was frequently evident in the busy kitchen. She became masterful at separating her own performance from the idiosyncrasies of the chefs.

She also learned how to **relax**—to "really" relax. She practiced breathing and relaxation tapes for many hours. This enabled Samantha's body and mind to remain calm in the heat of the moment.

When she was more able to achieve calmness, she could think more clearly and make better decisions.

Next, we worked on her **negative self-talk**. It was very important for Samantha to begin to recognize how she spoke to herself—which could take her into a downward spiral in no time at all. Then, she learned to change those thoughts into what I call "productive" thoughts, answering the question, "Will these thoughts take me to a useful and helpful place?"

We also looked at **fear**—acknowledging it and looking at it like her experience in her father's kitchen. She came to identify tightness in her chest, clammy hands, and an inability to think clearly as the same symptoms she experienced when her father was yelling at her or criticizing her. Over time she could replace those scary sensations with feelings of confidence and assuredness.

Lastly, Samantha learned to **visualize** the outcomes she wanted to accomplish. By using all her senses, she created powerful visualizations that exemplified the dignified, competent, reliable employee she was.

CHAPTER 3
Why This Work Is So Hard to Do Alone

Many people start the process of mindfulness and mental skills training by reading self-help books, listening to audiotapes, and watching videos. While these are all valuable resources, most people come to a point where they are not making any more progress. They are still plagued by some nagging patterns that don't seem to respond to all the information they have gathered.

These mindfulness practitioners are missing a very important ingredient: a guide or a mentor.

You see, real change happens in the unconscious, and as I mentioned, the unconscious, by its nature, the unconscious is unconscious. We have a limited view, "blind spots," to our unconscious unless we know the "language" of our unconscious and how to access material from it to make our unconscious *conscious*. Once our unconscious is made conscious, we can choose our behavior more thoughtfully.

A mentor knows the territory of the unconscious. She has been there before you and can see things that are still hidden from your view. A mentor will listen with "very big ears" and know exactly where you are, know where you need to go, and know how to guide you there.

Additionally, working on your own can be challenging and lonely. I consider personal growth work to be the work of the "Warrior." It takes courage and persistence to make friends with the part of you that you may not like and want to avoid. It's very nice to have support, somebody to encourage you along the way.

Another reason people fail doing this work alone is because motivation can be short-lived. We might start out on this journey with great enthusiasm and curiosity. How many times have you made resolutions, only to find you quickly return to your old ways? In the beginning, there's a lot of insight and understanding as to why you might behave the way you do. Real behavior change comes over time with practice and repetition—what I call "the long haul." Your mentor keeps you accountable and helps you stay on the path while you give your brain the time it needs to create new pathways that will lead to lasting change.

Lastly, your mentor is there to answer questions. We, humans, are complex. There are many layers to unravel and many dots to connect. With time and training, you will have access to these deeper parts of yourself but you will invariably save time, money, and heartache if you choose to work with an experienced mentor.

CHAPTER 4
How We Create Change

Over the course of my career, I have been obsessed with the question: "How do we change?"
And I mean, really change: so that our experience
of ourselves changes, not just our understanding. Throughout this book, you will find direct and
indirect references to Yoga Psychology, Buddhist
thought, Sports Psychology, Western Learning
Theory, Neuroscience, and Neuroplasticity. Ultimately, this information has been synthesized
and integrated through my own personal experience, as well as through observing successful
outcomes with hundreds of clients over thousands of hours.

Primarily, for our purposes here, we're going to
start with the concept of Neuroplasticity, which
is defined as "the brain's ability to change by
strengthening or weakening neural activity and

connections...to reorganize itself throughout life."[1] Psychologist Donald Hebb, the "Father of Neuropsychology" coined the phrase, "Neurons that fire together, wire together."[2] I interpret Hebb's statement to mean that, if we have a laser focus on a new behavior or habit, we will repeat the behavior over and over again. Via this repetition, we create new neural pathways that will, over time, become automatic. This is the foundational process by which the brain changes and re-organizes itself.

The second important concept we will focus on comes from Quantum Physics. This theory establishes that the very act of "watching" can change our reality. This concept is the basis of Mindfulness, which we will revisit and expand upon in a later chapter.

So, if we put these two laws together: Hebb's law—which works through the use of mental focusing and holding our attention, and the Quantum Physics law of "watching" in order to change matter, we end up with creating *new* neural firings and *new* neural connections, which translates into creating *new* behavioral habits, which it the

1 *http://www.medicinenet.com/script/main/art.asp?articlekey=40362*
2 *www.supercamp.com/what-does-neurons-that-fire-together-wire-together-mean/*

ultimate goal of this transformation.

If we want to create a new habit, we want the new desired behavior to "pop up"—to manifest—and the undesirable, or unwanted behavior to fade into the background.

For example, say I want to train myself to stretch in the morning before I eat my breakfast. For years, my habit is to get up, to get in the shower, then to have my breakfast. This is how I am wired. Every night I remind myself that I want to stretch in the morning. I get up, I shower, and then have my breakfast—only to remember when I'm having my breakfast that I didn't stretch. The third morning, I remember while I'm in the shower that I didn't stretch. I leave myself a note on the shower door...and by the fifth morning, I remember to stretch *before* I get into the shower. As I watch my behavior and leave myself clues, I get quicker and quicker at remembering my goal, which was to stretch, until I've created a new routine. Typically, it takes 30 to 40 days to create a new habit which means it takes 30 to 40 days to create the new neural pathway.

CHAPTER 5
Increasing Your Ability to Focus

So how, you might ask, does this neural rewiring relate to focus?

When we are laser focused on a task—which means we are mentally focusing, holding our attention, and watching—we engage our brain's wiring in assisting us to perform our desired out-come. In order to keep track of your progress, I recommend that you take a moment and think of a challenge that you would like to master by the time you finish working through this book. You might have several you would like to tackle, but I suggest you start with one. Once you see how the process works, you can take on other issues and apply the same principles. I advise you to be as specific as possible. The brain doesn't do well with multitasking when you want to increase your ability to focus. An abstract challenge might be more difficult than one that is more specific. For example, you might want to increase your ability to manage your anxiety in a certain situation. Specifically, you'd want to phrase this challenge as, "I want to be able to make a presentation and to feel relaxed, confident, and in command of my material." Or, you could say "I want to be able to stay focused on a project without my mind wandering all over the place." You could also pick something interpersonal such as: "I want to be able to control my anger when I encounter a particular person or a particular situation."

Now that you have your goal in mind, let's look at how to accomplish it. To change our behavior or to create a new habit, we need to break the behavior down into manageable chunks. To start, we need to recognize what we are already doing. Therefore, all behavior change begins with *awareness*, *awareness*, and *awareness*.

If we want to become laser-focused, we need to become aware of when we are *out* of focus so that we can then bring ourselves back into focus. This first exercise will begin to train your mind to focus while also helping you recognize when you're out of focus, so you can re-direct your attention back to the task at hand.

In the next chapter, we'll be talking more about meditation and the different ways you can practice it. However, this meditative exercise is foundational in beginning to build those new neural pathways that will help you to focus in any situation you encounter.

Exercise 1

Inhale through your nose and *exhale* through your mouth.

- Inhale for the count of 4

- Exhale for the count of 4

- Inhale for the count of 4

- Exhale for the count of 6-8

- Inhale for the count of 4

- Exhale for the count of 10-12

- Repeat

Every time your mind wanders and you get distracted, go back to the beginning of the exercise and start again. You want your whole mind to be flooded with counting your breaths.

Notice how you feel when you start the exercise. Then, notice how you feel after your practice.

27

Jot down some notes about your observations throughout this experience in a journal.

I always tell my clients that they cannot get to that place of inner calm without a regular "practice." Now that you have a basic understanding of how the brain allows us to establish new habits via neural pathways, you can appreciate why repetition and practice are the foundations of behavioral change.

CHAPTER 6
Meditation

The breathing exercise we did in the last chapter, counting our breath, was a specific kind of meditation which we will be talking about in this chapter.

There are many different definitions and kinds of meditation, but for our purposes here we going to define meditation as **focused concentration**. This definition means that when we are hyper-focused on one thing, there are several processes that happen in the brain which have the potential of taking us to the quiet, serene place that people associate with meditation.

However, there's a big misconception about meditation that I want to clear up. I frequently hear from people, "I'm not a good meditator," or I can't meditate." Is that you? Can you relate to that? What these folks mean is that when they sit down to meditate, their mind wanders and they are not able to keep it quiet enough to reach a Zen-like state. The truth is that meditation is a practice. Therefore, even the act of just attempting to hold your focus builds the muscle—or the neural pathway—that *might* lead you to that quiet place.

Jack Kornfeld, a well-known Mindfulness meditation teacher, talks in his book *A Path with Heart,*[1] about practicing meditation as you would train a puppy: The mind wanders, you bring it back. The mind wanders, you bring it back. Just as you grab a puppy dog by the scruff of its neck when it runs away, you bring it back. It runs away, you bring it back. If you sit and do *just* that exercise with your brain...for 5 minutes to begin with...and then 10 minutes...over time, your mind will become quieter and quieter. I've been meditating for almost 40 years. Some days my mind is very quiet and some days it's like a war zone. No matter where my mind is at on a given day, it's all meditation that I am practicing.

Given the practice required to become used to meditation and the varied state of our brains from day-to-day, a big part of being able to master your emotions under pressure is to truly be with

---

1 Kornfeld, Jack. *A Path With Heart*, Bantam Books, New York, NY. 1993.

"what is" and make your choices from that place. Do not become attached to the outcome; you will only get frustrated and disappointed. When our reality is in one place and expectation is in another, we feel disappointed and frustrated with the outcome. If you give yourself permission to just *be with* the experience of "what is"...the process will take you there—wherever "there" is.

For those of you who are "doers"—action-oriented, goal-oriented people—meditation is often a difficult process. In spiritual work, the challenge is to just *allow*—to create the space for something new to arise. There's a saying that says, "From nothing, comes something." Do the practice; be patient and see what arises. Notice what you notice. "Watch" without judgment, without expectation. You will meet yourself, your obstacle, and your resistances. Just notice. Write down your observations in your journal. You will be able, over time, to witness your progress.

What you are receiving in this training are not only the tools to manage your emotions under pressure but also a broader education into what the spiritual journey of transformation is truly about.

The word "enlightenment" means to shine the light onto dark places. When you sit in meditation, you slow down. The brain slows down, and we get to "see" what's going on our subconscious mind. If you sit with an attitude of curiosity and just notice, you will learn a lot about yourself. It's like taking a flashlight into a dark cave:

"How interesting!"

"Look where my mind goes!"

"I'm ready to get up."

"Is it time yet?"

"Oh, where did that come from? I can't believe that's what I started thinking about!"

"What was I supposed to be focusing on?"

"Ooh, I don't want to think about that!"

These are just some examples of what might show up when you sit quietly and stop "doing."

Meditation practice has many, many benefits. In an article entitled "Benefits of Meditation," Giovanni Dienstmann named seventy-six benefits of meditation.[2] From many of the studies he reviewed, Dienstmann noted that meditating for 20 minutes a day over a period of several weeks was enough to show significant change in a person's

---

2 *http://liveanddare.com/benefits-of-meditation/*

brain scans.

These benefits are grouped into three main categories:

Emotional Well-Being

Super Mind

Healthy Body

So, we can see that meditation is good for the body, the mind, and the spirit.

I'm going to offer you a few different meditations to try out since we are all built differently. Some of us are more visual, some more auditory, and some more kinesthetic.

Exercise 2

We're going to start with a simple **breath awareness meditation**, which is like the one we did in the first module except you don't have to count your breaths.

Get comfortable. Sit in a comfortable chair with a straight back. Put your feet on the floor—uncrossed—and let your hands rest gently in your lap.

You can make two circles with your thumbs and forefingers and interlace them so you have a continuous flow of energy all through your body, but this is not a necessary requirement.

Begin to focus on your breath. Just notice the air gently moving in and out through your nostrils.

Take a few moments and enjoy settling into your chair, noticing your feet on the ground and how your body is sitting in the chair.

Continue to follow your breath...watching the rise and fall of your chest as you breathe in and out through your nostrils.

If your mind wanders, just bring it back to the breath.

Continue to do this breathing exercise for the next 5-10 minutes.

When you are finished, just sit and notice how you are feeling. Write down your observations in your journal.

Exercise 3

The second meditation is a **mantra meditation**, which uses two Sanskrit syllables that you say to yourself over, and over again. Many mantras are unique to individuals, given to us by a spiritual teacher. The one we are using here is a universal mantra and is appropriate for everyone.

Again, get yourself into a comfortable, seated position. Put your feet on the floor, make sure your back is straight and put your hands in your lap.

Begin by noticing your breath. Breathe in and out through your nostrils... and watch the rise and fall of your chest. Begin to say to yourself "so...hum." You can say it silently to yourself or you can say it out loud.

"So" on the inhalation

"Hum" on the exhalation

"So...hum"

"So...hum"

And when your mind begins to wander, bring it back

"So...hum"

"So...hum"

Repeat for the next 5-10 minutes

When you're done, notice how you feel. Write down your observations in your journal.

Exercise 4

The third meditation is *mindfulness meditation* where we become aware, or mindful, of that which catches our attention in the present moment.

We will be talking more about mindfulness in future chapters, but mindfulness is another kind of focused concentration. Again, there are many different types of mindfulness meditations, but for our purposes here, this is a good one to start with.

Begin by sitting comfortably with your feet on the floor and your hands gently resting on your lap.

Once again, begin by noticing your breath and the rise and fall of your chest. The operative word in this meditation is notice. Notice what catches your attention and just follow where your attention takes you. Your attention could be on sensations in your body, it could be on sounds that you hear from outside or inside your house, or it could be on the thoughts that run through your mind.

The task here is not to get engaged but just to take notice. Wait until the next sensation, sound, or thought arises to take notice of it. If you find yourself getting distracted or lost in thought, just start again by coming back to your breath.

Here is an example of the interior monologue that accompanies a mindfulness meditation:

I notice the sound of the train going by...I notice the sound of the cars and a bus outside...I notice the smell of the roses on my desk...I notice my shoulders feel tight...etc.

Start with five minutes and build up to ten minutes or more. When you are finished, notice how you feel and write down your observations in your journal.

Again, I have offered you three different meditations so you can see what resonates with you personally. Any one of these meditations could be your practice for a lifetime. When you commit to one practice and you repeat it over and over again, you are training your body and your mind at a deep level. You are building new neural pathways that create deeper and deeper grooves, which makes it easier and easier to get your mind into an altered state.

I have given you more here in these meditations than you can master in a short period of time. Remember that you will have these meditations to come back to after you have finished reading this book.

CHAPTER 7
Relaxation

So far in this book, you have been given an exercise to help you increase your ability to focus and three different meditations for you to experiment with. I suggest you try them all and then choose the one you would most like to continue with on a regular basis.

The value of choosing one exercise is that you will begin to establish those new neural pathways that will make it easier and easier, over time, to slip into a state of meditation. Again, focus and meditation means you will slow down your brain waves and quiet your mind. One of the greatest benefits of establishing focus or meditation is that it will make it easier for you to observe your thoughts and behaviors that sit just underneath the surface in your subconscious mind.

And when you have access to your subconscious

mind, you begin to understand yourself at a much deeper level. The world of feelings and the world of thought are two different operations. Many years ago (which will give you an idea how long I've been working with these concepts) I used to say thoughts and feelings are like "Windows" and "Dos." Some of you reading this book may not even know what I'm talking about here. What I'm saying is that thoughts and feelings are like "apples and oranges." They are both fruit but two very different species.

How cool would it be to be able to have both your conscious (thoughtful) and subconscious (feeling-oriented) minds communicating with one another? When these two parts of us are in synergy, life works.

Let me give you an example: Let's say you recognize you may be unhappy in your career but you don't have the faintest idea as to what you want to do about this unhappiness. The truth is that the subconscious part of you knows exactly what makes you happy, what you're good at, what kind of environment you thrive in and many other answers that might elude your conscious mind.

When you slow down the brain and ask the right questions, you might be amazed at the ideas and possibilities that "pop up"—seemingly out of nowhere. This idea brings us to the subject of **relaxation**, the **relaxation response**, and **resetting the nervous system**.

All the previous exercises in this book have the capacity to put you into a state of relaxation. The next exercise I'm offering here, if you practice it, can help you shift your nervous system quickly—sometimes in an instant.

Let's start with a brief explanation of how the nervous system works so you have an understanding of what you are working towards and why it's so important to your overall well-being to be able to relax *at will*. There are two parts to the nervous system—the sympathetic and parasympathetic. The sympathetic nervous system goes into action when the body and mind perceive danger. The sympathetic nervous system enacts that fight, flight or freeze response that we commonly associate with stress. Depending on the level and duration of the stress, the symptoms may become more apparent and debilitating. For our fundamental purposes here, though, when we are in situations we perceive are out of our control (and that's my definition of stress—the *perceived* amount of control we have or don't have), we begin to release cortisol, adrenaline and other stress hormones.

41

Ideally, when the danger is over, the body returns to the parasympathetic nervous system—which is the one that says, "Life is good. I have money in the bank. I can slow down and relax." However, the problem is, in our culture, we rarely relax. We rarely get to that deep state of relaxation and renewal. With constant stress hormones running through us, our immune system becomes compromised and we become susceptible to stress-related diseases.

So again, we want to train our bodies and our minds to calm down, to stop the adrenaline flow, to think more clearly, and to choose the appropriate behavior that makes us feel good about ourselves. Achieving this calmness is really what being "in control" of our lives looks like.

Exercise 5

The first relaxation exercise in this chapter involves learning how to do a **yogic breath**, or what we call a **three-part breath**. The best way to do this exercise is to lie down on the floor. If your lower back needs more support, put a pillow under your knees. Get comfortable and put your hands on your belly.

The first part of the breath is to breathe in through your nostrils while allowing your belly to rise. This inhale is counter-intuitive and not the way we generally breathe so it might feel weird. You'll know you're doing the breath correctly if your hands are rising with the inhalation and falling with the exhalation of your breath as you breathe in and out through your nostrils. Imagine that your belly is a bellows that fills up with air and then deflates. This exercise may also make you feel like when you're full and can't hold your stomach in. Many women are well-practiced in holding in their stomachs. I'm suggesting here that you let it all go. You are bringing your breath into the first register.

Once you feel that you've got that first part of the breath mastered, move your hands up to your diaphragm—the second register. Now you're going to breathe into the belly and then into the diaphragm. Again, this process may be easier said than done. Just be patient and gentle with yourself.

Once you're able to smoothly bring the breath into the first and second registers, put one hand on your belly and one on your upper chest. Now you're going to breathe into your belly, into your diaphragm, and all the way up into your upper chest. Then, you'll let your belly collapse, then your rib cage, and then your upper chest.

Let all the air out before you take the next breath in.

Keep doing this breathing exercise for five minutes at first, then for ten minutes. Again, your mind might wander. Just bring your thoughts back to your breathing and start over again. When you are finished, turn and lie down onto one side and get up very slowly. You might feel sleepy or dizzy. You have just brought a lot of oxygen into your system—much more than it is used to.

Once you feel like you "have" the yogic breath mastered, you can do it sitting up. I asked you to practice lying down at first simply because it's easier to learn the exercise this way.

This breathing exercise has been a lifesaver for me—literally:

Twelve years ago, I was diagnosed with breast cancer. For the doctor to do a biopsy, they needed to insert a wire into my breast, but they couldn't use anesthesia. Every time they came close to me with that wire, I got nauseous and felt like I was going to faint. After the fifth attempt, I told the nurse to let me lie down on the floor so I could do my yogic breathing. She agreed... and after about five minutes I was in a deep state of relaxation. I told her when I was ready and that they could proceed. Honestly,

I did not feel one thing during the procedure.

If you practice this breath repeatedly, you will train your body and your mind to shift from the sympathetic to the parasympathetic nervous system quickly. In medical terms, they call this breathing-related shift between nervous systems your **heart rate variability** which is a good indicator of the level of stress on your heart. The more you're operating in the parasympathetic nervous system, the less stress on the heart.

Thus far, I have given you several ways to calm yourself down. I realize that there's a lot presented here and that you can only do one practice at a time. This book is intended to serve as an introduction to the world of stress management and I want you to find what resonates with and works for you.

Which one of these relaxation practices are you willing to commit to doing long-term? Be sure to spend time on each one. Then, pick one to repeat every day for the first month. You can also begin your chosen meditation practice with a few minutes of yogic breathing which will get you centered and make it easier to "sit."

One of my goals in writing this book, in addition to teaching you how to maintain a sense of calm in stressful situations, is to teach **confidence**. When you're sure you can keep your cool, you're more likely to take on more challenges, to play a bigger game, and to reach for goals that you might have previously thought were unattainable.

CHAPTER 8
Mindfulness Training

In this chapter, we're going to look at Mindfulness training and how we can incorporate it into our daily lives. Mindfulness is a mental state achieved by focusing one's awareness on the present moment, while calmly acknowledging and accepting one's feelings, thoughts and bodily sensations. In Chapter 5, I gave you a Mindfulness Meditation where you noticed whatever thoughts, feelings, or bodily sensations appeared, without becoming engaged in them. Now, in this chapter, we are expanding our use of mindfulness, not only when we are sitting in meditation, but in our feelings and bodily sensations throughout the day. By becoming increasingly aware of our thoughts, we become better and better observers of ourselves.

One of the most common complaints I hear from people is that they "know" they should behave differently or "want" to behave differently, but that the "how" to really *change* escapes them. For example, I have a client who is in sales and loves helping people with the product he is offering. He's a sensitive guy and "knows" that along with being a salesman, he has to get used to people saying "no." Even though he "knows" that he's supposed to be able to handle hearing "no," he interprets it as rejection. He can't control his feelings and frequently ends up at the end of the day feeling down and badly about himself.

The way that we would use *mindfulness* in this situation is by becoming aware—to have him become aware of his thoughts and belief systems about being a salesman, what his body feels like when someone says "no," and how he interprets those feelings.

You see, before we can change anything, we need to have a starting point. If you're at work and there's a problem in your business, you dissect it, look at all the variables, and decide on how to solve it. The same principle is true of our behavior. What people frequently do is *internalize* a situation and think that there is something wrong with them. Then, they go down a path that leads them to feel worse, with no useful information gathered as for how to change the situation. So, the most important aspect of being mindful is to look at your behavior with *non-judgmental* awareness. Your feelings are neither good nor bad, they just are. Acknowledging our thoughts and feelings with non-judgmental awareness gives us an opportunity to analyze a situation, identify the problems, and come up with good solutions.

Exercise 6

If we go back to Chapter 4, where we talked about Hebb's Law and quantum physics, what we are doing here is focusing our attention—or shining the light on those dark places, slowing down the process so we can assess what is *really* going on and then choosing new thoughts and behaviors that will result in building new neural pathways.

This exercise is to *notice* your thoughts, feelings, and bodily sensations throughout the day. Notice when you're feeling anxious, sad, frustrated, happy, exuberant. Notice what's happening inside of you.

Where are you feeling these feelings? If you practice mindfulness in this way, I expect that you might have some "aha" moments. You may notice that your behavior runs in patterns and you may begin to see that similar situations bring up similar and predictable thoughts and feelings.

I'm not asking you to change anything right now. I'm only asking you to notice what you notice. Then, spend some time writing down your observations in your journal over the coming days and weeks.

CHAPTER 9
Belief Systems

For you to become masterful at managing your emotions under pressure, you need to account for the mind, the body, and their interrelationship.

In the last four chapters, we spent a lot of time looking at the body and how to calm the nervous system by meditating, relaxing, and breathing. We also talked about noticing and watching our thoughts by being mindful. I specifically requested that you not worry about changing anything but just notice your thoughts with nonjudgmental awareness. This practice gave us a starting point to "see" what's really going on in your subconscious mind when we slow things down and get the opportunity to take a good look.

In this chapter, we're going to examine your belief systems and how they powerfully influence your behavior. After you've done a soul-searching investigation of your belief systems, in the next chapter, we'll work on choosing your thoughts so they align with your beliefs and practicing turning negative self-talk into what I call "productive thinking."

So, let's get started:

The best definition of belief systems I found is that, "Belief systems are the stories we tell ourselves to define our personal sense of 'reality.' Every human being has a belief system that they utilize, and it is through this mechanism that we individually, 'make sense' of the world around us."[1]

In his article, "Science, Faith and Belief Systems," Adam Gerhard talks about two kinds of belief systems: one is scientifically-based and the other is faith-based. In **scientifically-based belief systems**, science is used to build "evidence" that a particular belief is true. Since it is accepted knowledge that individuals can bring bias to a situation, through observation, experiment, and prediction, science requires a strict definition of terms and conditions and demands that any evidence is subjected to *trials* and *independent verification*. We see this verification process in the

---

1 Adam, Gerhard. Science, Faith and Belief Systems. Science 2.0, September 2011.

52

medical community and its strict adherence to clinical trials. Much of the debate between complementary and allopathic (or prescription-based) medicine surrounds this issue. It's not enough to *believe* that energy healing works. Many skeptics want physical proof that is backed up by evidence-based science.

In contrast, **faith-based belief systems** are mental constructs that *lack evidence*. Faith-based belief systems are unequivocally based on the *lack of evidence* or *evidence that may be impossible to collect*. So how does this information relate to our personal, transformational growth? We not only have one belief system, we have many of them. They are primarily unconscious and they rule us: frequently without us even being aware. We acquire our belief systems from our parents, our teachers, our friends, and the media. When our belief systems are unexamined, we may be living with constructs that are outdated, childlike, and potentially destructive.

Let me give you a few examples of subconscious belief systems. Racial bias is one of those blatant belief systems that perpetuates war and suffering. Yet, if you asked someone *why* he or she holds racist beliefs, they couldn't give you a rational answer. Somewhere along the path of their development, they adopted this way of thinking as the unequivocal truth despite its impossibility to prove.

On a sillier note, my mother told me that Heinz Ketchup was the best ketchup around. Do I know whether or not that's the truth? Of course not. Yet, I believe it's the best brand and that's the only ketchup I ever buy.

Then, there are belief systems that *positively* guide our lives and I certainly wouldn't want you to give them up. For example, The Golden Rule: "Do unto others as you would have them do unto you," has been a foundational belief I was taught by my parents and which I passed on to my three children.

Our belief systems guide every aspect of our behavior: how we parent, who we marry, our politics, our food choices, everything. So don't you think it's a good idea to examine these beliefs *carefully* and *consciously* and decide which ones are ours? To decide which ones we want to keep and which ones belong to someone else that we've unconsciously adopted as our own? To reject belief systems that no longer serve us?

The way we can begin to recognize our unconscious belief systems is by being mindful and listening to our "shoulds."

I should buy Heinz ketchup.

I should treat others like I want to be treated.

I should exercise.

And so on.

Exercise 7

Step 1 Take out a pad of paper and on each page, head it with one of the following:

Work

Family

Romantic relationships

Friends

Physical/Health

Spiritual

Step 2 Over the course of the week, every time you think of a "should" in any of these areas, write it down on the appropriate page. This process may be a bit of an eye opener.

For example,

I should work 40 hours a week.

I should marry a man or woman who shares my religious beliefs.

I should eat only organic food.

You get the idea.

Step 3 After three days of diligently observing your belief systems and writing them down, look over your list and mark next to each one who holds this belief.

For example:

If I've said, "I believe that I should exercise three times a week," I recognize it was my father's belief, my doctor's belief, and my belief.

Or, "I believe that an extended family should live in the same neighborhood," was my mother's belief.

Step 4 After you have identified the origin of these beliefs as best you can, go through the list again and ask yourself: "Do I want this belief for myself at this time of my life?" and put a "yes," or a "no" next to each item.

Step 5 After you have consciously identified the beliefs that you want in your life, go down the list again and say the statements that you clearly want to keep slowly and consciously, with your whole emotional body along for the ride: "I choose the belief that"....and fill in the blanks.

For example,

"I choose to follow the Golden Rule in my life."

" I choose to exercise three times a week."

Be very aware, that when you make these choices you are making a commitment to yourself. I suggest you only accept those beliefs that you are willing to whole-heartedly commit yourself to.

Make this exercise a sacred ceremony.

Examining and working with your belief systems in this way is a very important element of transformational work. This work requires your full commitment but can dramatically change your life for the better.

CHAPTER 10
Overcoming Negative Thinking

In the last chapter, we spent a lot of time looking at belief systems. If you remember, these are the thought constructs that shape our thoughts and our behavior. Because belief systems are frequently unconscious, they can rule us without our even realizing it. I hope you spent a good bit of time examining your beliefs and choosing only those beliefs that work for you in your current life. If you did the exercise thoughtfully, you might find that you are shifting your behavior to match what you say you want for yourself.

I remember that when I first did this exercise I chose to commit myself to exercising three times a week. If I missed a day, instead of beating myself up, I just remembered that exercising was something I chose to do and I re-organized my time in order to make it happen.

The reason we started with belief systems is because I wanted you to be sure that what you *say* you want and what you *do* are connected. When our conscious mind and our subconscious mind are in alignment, we are more likely to manifest our dreams, goals, and desires. For example, in my commitment to exercise three times a week, I ultimately wanted the physical result of what exercise could do for me. I wanted to keep my weight stable, I wanted to get strong, and I wanted to be healthy. If I didn't follow through with my commitment to myself, I wasn't a bad person; I just wouldn't get the result that I said I wanted.

The mind has a natural propensity for offering us negative thoughts. We are hardwired to look for danger and threats. Otherwise, our ancestors would not have survived. Therefore, we can frequently get lost in flood of negativity that takes us down a nasty spiral. When we spiral, not only do we feel bad about ourselves, we also get further and further away from our goals. So, if you want your life to be happier and your brain to be healthier (because negative thinking sets off stress hormones in the brain), you need to take on this project with serious commitment.

There are a number of subtle ways that our negative thinking takes us out of control over ourselves. By being mindful of what we are feeling and what we are thinking, we get closer and closer to having control over our minds than rather than our minds having control over us.

Here are a few examples of what we call "cognitive distortions"—unconscious patterns that we have developed as ways to protect ourselves and that are still operating under the radar. Cognitive distortions can amplify our negative thoughts. See if you can relate to any of these:

Over-Generalization: Reaching a general conclusion based on a single incident.

For example, you muster up the courage to ask a new acquaintance out to lunch and they decline. You walk away thinking that no one will want to be your friend.

People who think like this have a tendency to make a mountain out of a molehill, think in absolutes, and jump to conclusions based on insufficient data.

Could this be you?

One of the ways to work with over-generalization is to ask yourself: Is my conclusion rational or irrational? This is a great question to remember, for it helps to put things in their proper perspective.

The next example is what we call **Polarized Thinking**.

People have a tendency to look at the world in absolutes:

Things are either right or wrong, good or bad, always or never.

As you pay attention to your own thinking, ask yourself: Is this me?

This is the kind of thinking that children do. They like things to be simple so they can feel like they have some control. But, the truth is that life is complicated and we live in a world of coexisting opposites. As we mature, we become more able to hold these opposites. Yes, the world is both good and bad, there are things which are both right and wrong, and so on.

How about **Catastrophizing**?

We'll talk more about this concept when we get to the chapter on fear, but when you think that the worst possible scenario can and will happen, you create a situation in both your mind and your body that leads to anxiety, apprehension, and worry. Notice whether your vocabulary is filled with "What ifs." "What if this happens? What if that happens?" Notice what happens to your body when you follow those questions.

And how about **Mind Reading**? Do you ever say to someone, "I know just what you're thinking?"

Making assumptions without verification can get us into a lot of trouble. The truth is that we can never know what someone is thinking without them validating our assumption. We can have strong intuition that we are right, but strong intuition is a just a good hunch—not always the truth.

So, be sure to phrase your "mind reading" words to others in the form of a question. "I'm wondering if this is what you're thinking...is that true?"

There are many more cognitive distortions we could explore, but the important point I want to emphasize is that you should notice your patterns of thinking. Do you frequently feel misunderstood or hurt by others? These feelings are good indicators that the way you're thinking is responsible for that downward spiral, rather than others who are purposefully out to hurt you.

Once we have examined our belief systems, adjusted them to our present life and noticed our thought patterns, we're ready to change some of those thoughts into what I call *productive* thinking.

Exercise 8

Observe your thoughts. Notice how you talk to yourself. If you run into a situation where you feel uncomfortable, reflect on your thinking. How did I just talk to myself? Did I call myself names? Would I talk to my worst enemy the way I spoke to myself? Does this kind of thinking take me to a good place? Write down your observations. Additionally, write down anything else you notice throughout this process.

In the next chapter, we will work more specifically on exactly what to do with these thoughts so they take you to someplace useful and helpful, rather than down the rabbit hole.

CHAPTER 11
From Negative Thinking to Productive Thinking

In the last chapter, we examined several cognitive distortions, which are patterns of thinking that you learned early in your life and continue to exhibit into adulthood, without even realizing it. People will say, "I can't help it, it's just who I am," or "this is just me." The truth is, these are behaviors and attitudes you learned; they are not necessarily who you are. You can't change your character traits, but you can certainly change your attitudes and your behaviors.

In this training, we are not just learning mental skills, we are also working through layers of conditioning that can lead to real transformation. When I think of the word "transformation," it's not about becoming or transforming into someone else but, rather, about coming home to you: your authentic self. Being a master under pressure means being the best *you* that *you* can be.

So now that we've looked at your belief systems and your patterns of behavior that you no longer want, let's get down to the nitty-gritty of transforming your self-talk.

You may have heard people talk about "positive self-talk." From my experience, just changing your thoughts into a positive statement without doing much of the work that we've just done in previous chapters doesn't always work. As I've mentioned several times, your conscious mind and your subconscious mind have to be in agreement in order to manifest long-lasting change.

Let's say you're struggling at work either with a fellow employee or a client who really bugs you. Every time you need to interact with this person, you get triggered, either by something they say, or by a look, or even by their tone of voice. When this triggering happens, our most natural tendency is to either want to avoid the person or to keep the time we spend together at a bare minimum.

But what if we looked at this person as a gift, as a teacher, or as someone who has come into your life for a reason?

If you remember, we previously talked about the fact that we create our own reality. People are simply mirrors through which we can examine our own thoughts and beliefs. It's always about us, not about them.

I'll give you an example. I had a situation where I needed some work done for my business and someone offered to help. I was delighted to have the assistance but, as time went on, our relationship soured. The person helping me had underestimated the time it would take to get the project done and I was scrambling to meet his deadlines. I was picking up his resentment, but I also needed his help at the price we had agreed upon.

Now, I could have spent a lot of time focusing on how angry I was with him and how his attitude made me feel. Instead, I worked with two axioms:

1. I create my own reality, so no one "makes me feel" anything. I allow these feelings to happen.

2. Therefore, it follows that if I create my own reality, I need to look at how got myself into the situation and what I can learn from the situation.

In this way, I can put myself back in charge of my

life and use a frustrating situation as my teacher.

If I go down the road of holding on to being angry with a person, I only get to feel bad. My adrenaline goes up, my muscles get tight, and I still haven't solved the problem.

Instead of holding on, I notice my anger; I don't ever deny it. Then, I decide what I want to do about my anger. Is it worth confronting this person? Will that help alleviate my negative feelings?

Is it truly better for me to keep quiet and just finish the project? Or, should I call it quits and find someone else to help me?

You see, now I have created options for myself. Each one of these possible solutions can produce something useful for me. I'm back in charge of my life. I'm not a victim. I get to choose.

Here's another example I think you'll be able to relate to:

I need to send out a package. It's a Saturday morning. I get up, get dressed and go to the post office, only to find that they're closed. My first reaction is to be annoyed. But, again, if I hold on to that negative thought, my mood goes downhill. *I don't want a negative spiral to happen.*

So, I recognize my annoyance. I ask myself if holding onto this feeling is taking me to a good place. (It isn't.) So, I look for another way to think about my situation.

Well, I didn't look to see whether the Post Office was open or not. Now I know that they open later on Saturdays and I won't make that mistake again.

This may seem like a trivial example, but once you start noticing how many times distressing situations and inconveniences dictate your mood, you begin to find it fun and powerful that you can shape your response to many of life's surprises.

In my career, I've spent a lot of time working with tennis players. As many of you know, tennis is heavily dependent upon a strong mental game. One of the biggest lessons a player can learn is that while they can have negative thoughts running through their minds, they can also quickly recognize that these are "just thoughts." As we talked about in our mindfulness training, you can see these thoughts float by. You do not have to engage in these thoughts and you certainly don't have to believe they are true.

This way of thinking is an eye-opener for many athletes and performers and it can be an eye opener for you, too.

To continue building on the work you have done, thus far, I want you to continue noticing your thoughts. If you find that your mood is sinking because of something that has happened, ask yourself:

1. How am I feeling about this situation?

2. How am I thinking about this situation?

3. Do my thoughts take me to a good place?

4. If not, how can I change them to produce something useful for me?

Once we recognize that we create much of our own suffering, we are also liberated by the fact that we can find our own way out of such situations.

Please write down your observations as you process triggering events and interactions so you can continue to track your progress toward an unstoppable mindset.

CHAPTER 12
Managing and Transforming Fear

Just the word "fear," can bring up an uncomfortable bodily sensation. Fear is a powerful emotion that can rule us if we do not examine it.

As with everything else we have worked on in this book, we are looking to acquire skills that put us back into the driver's seat of our own lives.

Fear arises inside of us when a part of our brain, the amygdala, picks up a sense of danger. The amygdala is like a sentry on alert 24 hours a day, 365 days a year. The amygdala is also part of the limbic system—or our emotional brain—that holds memories of past dangers and traumas—big and small.

If we go back to our definition of stress, you might remember that we said it's based on the amount of control we perceive we have or don't have. Stress is a physical, chemical and emotional response to our perception of those situations that we deem out of our control. Underneath those perceptions is the feeling of fear. Fear manifests itself in many different ways. Sometimes we can recognize that we're scared. We feel jittery, our hearts are racing, our hands get sweaty, our muscles tighten up, and our thoughts become jumbled. In these moments we can usually name what makes us feel afraid.

Then, there are other fears that we have developed during childhood. These fears are not so apparent until we start digging for them. These fears are frequently the anchors that weigh us down and keep us from being all that we can be. We can call such feelings primary fears, life themes, or the stories we have told ourselves to make sense of our world.

My preferred list of fear types comes from the Persephone Center for Shamanic Energy Medicine.[1]

See if you can find yourself on this list:

The **fear of inadequacy** shows up as feeling like you're not good enough. Have you ever wanted to do something but then said to yourself, "I don't know enough. If I take just take one more course

---

1 *https://www.persephonecenter.com*

or get another degree or certification, then I'll know enough"?

The **fear of losing control** stems from how we all like to feel in charge of our lives. Being in charge makes us feel safe. Many people think that if they can control events, time, or other people that that will give them the sense of safety they are looking for. In my experience (because I'm personally a reformed control freak), I have had a difficult time tolerating uncertainty. Previously, if I didn't know what was coming next, I felt anxious. Leaving things to chance was a scary business for me. I had to learn how to tolerate uncertainty because that's what life requires.

The **fear of being worthless** or of **not being valued** means that somehow, no matter what you do or what you say, you think people don't value you or your opinion.

The **fear of change** means not being prepared for or wanting to change.

We can see this fear in people who are commitment-phobic because if they make a commitment to anything or anyone, they may also need to change. However, living requires us to move out of our comfort zone of familiarity. It never ceases to amaze me how long people can stay in uncomfortable situations because they're afraid of change. Sometimes, this fear can last a lifetime.

The **fear of lack or want** is a fear of not having enough. These folks come from a background of scarcity as opposed to a background of abundance. There is never enough of something for these people: not enough money, not enough love, or not enough attention.

The **fear of vulnerability** is a fear of being judged, criticized or ridiculed.

This was also a huge fear for me to overcome. When I was in high school, I wouldn't get up and dance. Even though I have good rhythm and I am a good dancer, the thought of other people watching me—and then my imagining that they would make fun of me—was more than I was willing to risk.

And lastly, the **fear of missing** out means having the sense that the grass is always greener in some other place or time—never being satisfied with where you are in the moment.

The interesting thing about these primary fears is that they usually don't feel like fear when you experience them. You do not necessarily feel afraid when you experience a primary fear. These fears can show up as procrastination, perfectionism, arrogance, stubbornness, self-deprecation, obsessive behaviors, greed, and other dysfunctional behaviors.

As I've been saying throughout this book, you cannot change anything until you acknowledge or identify what needs to change. Primary fears are often the root of what we need to change.

Exercise 9

I suggest you pause here and to take some time, go through the list of primary fears and see if you can identify where you fit. As for me, there were two main fears that checkered my childhood and adolescence. It wasn't until my late 20s that I began to recognize these patterns and work on changing them.

Now that you've identified your primary fear or fears, what I'd like you to do is pick one to work on first. I suggest that you pick a fear that is not too heavily loaded, just so you can build some skill and then tackle some of the more challenging fears and associated behaviors to overcome in the next round.

The most important thing to remember when you're working with your fears is that these are **thought constructs** you made up somewhere along the road of your development. These constructs are not "who" you are and they are not happening in the present. My goal in the next chapter is to help you clear these fears; right now we are simply identifying them and looking for their origins.

If at any time you feel overwhelmed or don't feel safe doing this exercise alone, you may want to engage the services of a trusted mentor who can guide you through the process. Take good care of yourself and be sure to ask for support if you feel you need some assistance.

Now that you've named the fear you would like to work on, see if you can find where it lives in your body. Memory gets stored both in the brain and in the body. Creating a relationship between your mind and your body means creating a shortcut to your subconscious mind.

Pause here for a moment to see if you can find the place in your body where you hold memories of fear and pain—it could be anywhere. I had a client who felt fear in her legs. She had two older brothers who would chase her around their house and she would run away from them out of fear for her safety.

Just like we did in the mindfulness exercises, see

if you can just observe this part of your body. Notice the thoughts, sensations and/or images that might come up. You may also not experience anything. There is no right or wrong answer here. Now that you have a sense of where this fear lives, just notice it.

You'll want to do this exercise for at least 30 seconds to a full minute—or even longer if you're intrigued.

Lastly, you'll want to ask your body when else you have felt this feeling and wait for an answer. There's no thinking here; this is a process of allowing.

You might be getting flashes of memories. Again, these might be in images, words, and/or sensations. If you don't have any memories that appear, that's okay, too. Now, slowly go back in time, asking your body if it remembers when the earliest memory of this feeling appeared. Wait for an answer.

When you're finished with this exercise, write down your observations.

To help clarify this exercise, I'll give you an example from my own life:

I know that I don't like the feeling of being out

of control. I was recently audited by the Internal Revenue Service, which lead to an ultimate out of control feeling for me. Every time I would think about the audit, my shoulders would tighten up and my stomach would turn over. As I sat and observed this reaction, I remembered a time, many years before, when my ex-husband was being unfairly investigated by the IRS for fraud. All the scary images of that time surfaced, like a moving picture.

By watching and observing this drama, I realized that I was bringing all of those fears into my current audit. This insight helped me to become more rational. This was a different situation from my ex-husband and my books were in a lot better shape than his were so many years ago, before computers. This experience helped me to bring myself back to the present with a different perspective.

Just to let you know, there was no fraud—just many lessons to learn about my fears.

Take your time. Go through this fear exercise carefully and thoughtfully. Remember, if you run into any difficulty or have any questions, be sure to ask for help.

CHAPTER 13
Clearing the Fears

In this chapter, we're going to work on clearing our fears, which really means clearing the *energy* that perpetuates our fears. This chapter is jam-packed.

Previously, we looked at some of the fears that frequently sit underneath our most unwanted behaviors. We talked about how we might not recognize them as fears, but with a little digging, we could find that scary thought or feeling that stops us in our tracks. With a little more investigation, we discovered that we can even find the origins of these fears from early in our lives.

So, you might ask, what's the value in doing all this work? I truly believe that when you can name and identify your fears, you can use them as your greatest teachers.

In the last chapter, I talked about my fear of being vulnerable—of being afraid that people would make fun of me if I got up and danced. By taking the time to investigate the origin of that fear, I could challenge the veracity of it. I could take myself out of the irrational realm and bring my grown-up logic to the situation. Once I could see the reality of the situation, I could problem solve and choose the behaviors and thoughts that would best serve me.

I'm hoping by this point in the book you're seeing the beauty of how these puzzle pieces all work together:

Now that you've named the fearful feelings and where you can find them in your body, let's look at the next step.

I'm going to use the example of being vulnerable again if I were to get up and dance. In that example, I recognize that I don't like the way I'm feeling. Everyone is having fun and I'm not. I find the feeling in my body: my shoulders are tight, my stomach is uneasy, and my thoughts about myself are nasty.

I realize that I might not be able to clear those feelings in the moment, but I commit to myself to take the time the next morning to go deeper.

The next morning, I sit with those feelings, just like we talked about in the last chapter. I watch. I watch myself becoming even more uncomfortable as I relive the night before. However, there are some facts that I know about feelings:

1. Feelings are just sensations and thought constructs that we have created for a reason.

2. If I just watch my feelings and not attempt to stop them, they have an arc; or I think of it as a bridge. Initially, the feelings might become more intense and uncomfortable which is where and why most people cut them off. But, if we allow such feelings to run their course, they might reach a peak and then the intensity will decrease. This is also the time where insights appear.

This is one way we can clear a fear. Once we get to the other side of the feeling, we have opened new doors, so to speak. One of my teachers used to talk about the intelligence of the mind vs. the intelligence of the heart: two different kinds of intelligences. Real transformation happens in the heart. We can begin to have greater compassion for that fearful child part of us who is still unconsciously operating in the present, but who no longer serves us.

By taking the time to do this level of work, I could see the relationship between my fear of losing control of my tightly-wound self on the dance floor and my very challenging relationship with my controlling father.

In my experience, people get frustrated because they can't make the changes they want to make. They read books, listen to tapes, and go to workshops, but the changes they want to make still sometimes feel elusive. This elusiveness is because they don't understand how the brain and specifically, the subconscious mental work.

Our emotional side and our mental side operate very differently from each other and they are in different locations in the brain. If these two systems are not in alignment or agreement, change will not happen since they will cancel each other out.

If you go back to the work we did in Chapter 9 where we talked about belief systems, I asked you to be sure that you wanted a particular belief in your life at present. Many times, we say we want something to go away but when faced with the reality of what we might have to give up, we change our minds. For example, let's imagine that you were bullied when you were younger and that every time you thought about going to school, you would get a stomachache. When you felt this way you got to stay home from school and get a lot of attention from your parents. So, being sick got attached to feeling loved. For you to embrace health, therefore, there might be remnants of this connection and getting well might, unconsciously, be scary. The body/mind will not let go of this construct until it is sure that you have another safe way of getting love and attention.

We call this situation a double bind. You want to move forward, but if you do there's a part of you that must face some unwanted, scary feelings.

So, in clearing your fears, you need to be sure that your whole self wants the new behaviors. If you don't find that agreement, you need to go back and do a little more investigation. You must keep in mind that these behaviors were developed for good reasons. Therefore, it is critical that you be kind and compassionate with yourself when doing this work.

If you find some resistance to moving on, you'll want to ask yourself a few questions and wait for the answers—questions like:

"What are you scared of?

"How come you're holding on to this feeling?"

"Why are you here?"

"What purpose do you serve?"

"What are you here to teach me?

Remember, if you want more lasting results, this work must precede you replacing primary fears with the positive, wanted feelings.

When working with your feelings, remember that feelings are energy. Again, the energy of a particular feeling lives both in our brain and in our body. The energy of a well-honed habit moves very quickly through our system, most times completely out of our awareness. To make the changes you want to make, you have to slow the energy down, which means you have to get some distance from the feeling so you can observe it and then create the desired shifts. This nature of feelings is the reason why the practice of mindfulness is so important to cultivate. For a metaphor: Imagine that you are slammed up against a brick wall. You can't really see the whole wall, just that little bit that's in front of your eyes. But, if you step back and remove yourself from that narrow focus, you see a much bigger picture.

The next few exercises will begin to give you the

distance you need to slow the feeling process down and disconnect you from the intensity of your feelings. We don't usually make very good decisions when we're in the heat of the moment.

Let's say you discover that one of your big fears is about the scarcity of money and you recognize that it's not really about the amount of money you have, because that fear of loss and scarcity never goes away, no matter how much money is in the bank. Additionally, every time you think about your bank account, the only thing you see is the balance going down.

I got this exercise from a great healer named Brandy Gillmore, and she calls it SIT 101 ™ which stands for sensory integration.[1] All these exercises are based on the neuroscience I discussed in Chapter 5. When we bring in our five senses; visual, auditory, kinesthetic, olfactory, and gustatory into our processing, we enhance our ability to reprogram our brains. Remember: neurons that wire together, fire together.

Exercise 10

Pick a fear that you would like to clear, one you know it's time to let go.

---

1 *http://www.brandygillmore.com*

Now, imagine a picture of you, being scared, are in front of you.

For example, I'm imagining an image of myself looking at my bank account and feeling that my stomach is sinking.

Once you have the sensation of your fear, rate the intensity of the sensation on a scale from 1 to 10; 1 being no intensity at all and 10 being very intense.

Now, imagine the number 1 in between you and that image.

And the number one is filled with lemons. And then keep counting, with each number filled with some other colors or objects.

For example, the number 2 is bright red with white pompoms, the number 3 is filled with fir trees and you can smell the smell of Christmas, the number 4 is filled with orange flags, and so on.

Count to 10 and then stop. Check the intensity of the feeling that you started with on that scale of 1 to10. Notice whether the intensity has changed or not. If it hasn't changed or if it's gone down only slightly, keep going. Check yourself again at 20. You can go as far as you need to in order for the sensation of the fear to diminish. See if you can get your 1 to 10 rating down to zero. I have found this exercise to be extremely effective in neutralizing the energy of a particular emotion I find uncomfortable.

Again, once I can get to that place where I'm no longer triggered by the situation, I'm ready to add in the feeling that I do want. We will be doing this work in the next chapter on visualization. For now, you want to practice simply acknowledging your fears and clearing them.

Using the same example of the fear of lack of money, I begin to imagine what I will feel like when my bank account goes up. I begin to feel like I expect it to show up. I can add any number of images and thoughts and feelings.

In summary, there's a lot of information here and a lot to tackle. Ultimately, you have two ways to work on clearing your fears: One method is to sit and watch your fears rise and then diminish and the other is to practice the counting I just described. Both methods are extremely effective.

There are many other techniques; more than we can cover here, but the basic fact you want to remember is to create distance between yourself and your unwanted feelings. Then, you have the luxury of choosing new thoughts and behaviors.

CHAPTER 14
Creating Powerful Visualizations Part 1

In the last two chapters, we worked on acknowledging and clearing our fears. I realize this is an ongoing process. Hopefully, though, you now have some tools in your toolbox you can return to over, and over, again as you get better and better at naming your fears and clearing them. Now that you have created space for new feelings to come in, you are ready to learn how to create powerful visualizations.

I remember when I was starting my first private psychotherapy practice and had no clients. Every morning I would imagine that my phone was ringing, I would pick it up and imagine someone on the other line saying, "Hello...my name is so and so and I was referred to you by so and so and I would like to make an appointment." After a while, every time I had an opening, I would visualize that image and say that phrase myself, and, honestly, the phone would ring—sometimes in minutes and almost always within two weeks. I became a firm believer in the power of visualization!

One fact about visualization is that your body, your brain, and your nervous system can be programmed like a computer to do what you want, provided you know how to program them. Let's say that one of your goals is to achieve peak performance in an aspect of your life. There are several requirements needed to make this goal happen and now we'll start to see how visualization fits into this paradigm. For a specific example, let's imagine that you'd like to become an expert speaker. Public speaking is a skill that requires knowledge, practice, and repetition. Great speakers also appear very relaxed, even though we know that public speaking is up there as one of the greatest fears of many people. So, in order to become a great speaker, we have to know our subject very well and also the nuances of how to deliver a great speech. These needs are where the practice and repetition come in. When we practice a skill over, and over again—whether it's public speaking, learning to play an instrument, or learning a new sport, we teach our body and the mind the skills involved, Such repetition creates new pathways in the brain.

When we get to perform a skill: give our speech, play the piano at a recital, or join a sports team, over time we begin to trust that the body and the mind have learned the skill because it has become embedded in the subconscious mind. Now, the question is, "When we're performing, what do we do with the other part of our mind which is conscious – the one we have direct access to?"

This part of our mind is where most people get hung up. They spend their time *while* performing worrying about how they're doing. They get into that negative self-talk space instead of *trusting* that they have taught their subconscious mind well and believing they only need to focus on the task at hand.

Going back to wanting to be a great public speaker, if you practice your speech over, and over, again you have taught your subconscious mind the material content. Now, when you're speaking you need to focus on your speaking skills such as connecting with your audience, having eye contact, using gestures, and so on. You must trust that your content will be there for you; you have practiced well and it will lead to a great performance!

Here's another example from my experience in working with tennis players: Practice sessions are their time to learn and practice new skills, such as strokes and footwork. During a match, many players get lost in bemoaning their performance on the previous point. However, game time is not the time to work on practicing their strokes. There are actually only a few things a player needs to focus on during a match: making quick corrections, recognizing their opponent's weaknesses, and their strategy for beating them, point by point by point.

Here are a few more important facts about visualizations before you start creating your own :

1. The conscious mind, which is usually a left-brain function, is associated with thinking, reasoning, analyzing, and category sorting.

2. The subconscious mind is more associated with the right brain and many ongoing physiological processes such as heart rate, temperature regulation, proper functioning of internal organs, and running many of our habitual patterns.

3. The subconscious mind is impersonal; it will do as you program it to do. If you program your subconscious mind with negativity, it will do

your bidding. Conversely, if you program your mind for success, it will perform successfully.

Therefore, in order to be successful at creating powerful visualizations you will want to think about programming each part of your brain appropriately. You'll want to practice your skill many times, so it will be embedded in the subconscious mind. Then you should focus your conscious mind on the just those things that will help you achieve a great performance. In this way, your whole body and mind will be in sync.

You also must have a strong desire or purpose for your visualization to be successful. You must believe it's possible for you to attain what you want which goes back to our lessons on belief systems. You'll want to ask yourself: "Are all parts of me in agreement to make this visualization become a reality?"

Now that we have all the background information in place, you're ready to create a powerful visualization. In this instance, imagine you need to prepare for an important presentation. This presentation may be in front of a large audience, it may be to just one or two people at work, or it may even be making cold sales calls. No matter the situation, you want to be at your best.

Exercise 11

We're going to call this exercise a "pre-perfor-mance" visualization which will get your whole body and mind to ready make that "killer" pre-sentation.

Get into a comfortable seated position, with your back nice and tall and your feet firmly planted on the floor. Close your eyes if you like or keep a soft gaze with your eyes slightly opened.

Begin by noticing your breath, watching your chest rise and fall with every inhalation and exhalation.

Now, begin to bring to mind the presentation that you are preparing to give.

Notice your body: How do you feel? What sen-sations do you notice? What are your thoughts? Just listen.

Now, ask yourself, "What do I need to do to per-form my best?" The answer might be things like what time you want to get into bed the night be-fore or what time you need to wake up so that you're not rushed. What are you going to wear? What do you want to have for breakfast?

Watch yourself make all these preparations. Feel how well rested you are. Smell the breakfast you've made for yourself. Notice your insides—how do they feel? If you're not feeling those positive feelings you would like to feel, bring them in. Take your time.

Listen carefully to your inner thoughts: Are you offering yourself kind, supportive words? If not, change the words—as if you're your own cheering squad.

Then, take your time to see if there are any last-minute details you have to attend to. Finally, watch yourself gathering what you need, so you are ready to walk out the door.

Take your time to make all the necessary adjustments until you feel like a champion!

When you're ready, slowly bring your attention back to the chair you're sitting in, feeling your feet on the floor, your hands on your lap. Wiggle your fingers and toes and gently open your eyes.

This exercise is an example of mentally rehearsing a scene. There are other kinds of visualizations we will be talking about in the next chapter.

When you are creating your own visualizations, remember to imagine as if the scene you're imagining is in the present time and be sure to bring in as many of your senses as you can. By visualizing in the present with all your senses, your brain will accept your suggestion so that when you go to prepare on the day your event, it will feel like déjà vu.

CHAPTER 15
Creating Powerful Visualizations Part 2

In the last chapter, I gave you a breakdown of creating visualizations with some important facts to remember.

Specifically:

☐ You must have a strong desire or purpose for your visualization to be successful

☐ You must believe it's possible for you to attain what you want to attain

☐ You must be willing to accept and have the accomplishment which you are seeking

☐ You must imagine your visualization as if it's happening in the present

☐ You must bring as many senses as possible into your visualization

We also created a pre-performance visualization where you imagined that you were preparing for a big event in which you wanted to perform your absolute best.

In this chapter, we'll look at a few other kinds of visualizations. In addition, I'll give you some other ideas as to how to enhance your visualizations to make them even more powerful.

This next approach, called **Picturing the Desired Outcome**, was made famous by Tim Gallway in his book, *The Inner Game of Tennis*; where he pioneered a method of teaching brand new tennis players to play reasonably well in an hour.

Here are the steps he used:

1. He asked them to hit a ball over the net and observe what they did, without any judgment.

2. Then, he asked them to picture their desired outcome by mentally making the corrections they thought they needed.

3. Then, he asked them to hit the ball again; trusting that the subconscious mind would register the visualized image and that the body would know what to do.

4. Lastly, he asked them to calmly observe their

results again with no judgment—and then to picture their desired outcome again.

This was a process of calmly observing results and learning by trial and correction.

Exercise 12

What I suggest you do is pause for a moment and think of a skill that you have been wanting to learn or improve upon. This skill could be something physical, like a sport or playing an instrument; or, it could even be improving your communication skills. Whatever it is, I suggest you practice by using the Gallway method to improve your performance of this skill.

Here are the steps again:

Step 1 Observe your existing behavior

Step 2 Picture your desired outcome

Step 3 Let it happen! Trust the subconscious

Step 4 Non-judgmentally and calmly observe your results

Repeat.

The more you do this visualization method, the greater your learning will be. Remember, peak performance comes with practice and repetition.

Training and trusting your body will allow you to calm your mind.

You can also use visualization: when you are in the middle of performance. Let's imagine you are giving a presentation and you lose your focused mind. This situation happened to me when I was giving a Toastmaster's speech.

I had practiced the speech very well. Then, the night before giving my speech I decided I didn't like the opening and I changed it. Big mistake! When I got up to begin my speech, my mind went completely blank. It was a friendly audience and a learning environment so I just said: "Excuse me, I'm going to start over again." That kind of hiccup was okay in that situation, but it wouldn't have been too cool if I were getting paid thousands of dollars for my talk.

So, I needed to have a "tried and true" method that would help me to re-engage and get focused again if I were to I lose my concentration. I went back to my practice of yoga.

Exercise 13

There is a yoga pose called the Mountain Pose which you may want to try.

Stand up with your feet hip distance apart and

your posture nice and tall, with a straight spine You can imagine that there is a string that is pulling you up from the top of your head as if you were a marionette.

Now, engage the energy in your legs. Engage the area around the center of your pelvis (this is your power center) and raise your arms to the sky like you are standing tall and firm on the top of a mountain. This is a power pose.

If you focus on your feet and on your pelvis, you will bring your energy back into your body and quiet down the chatter or the flightiness in your mind.

For me, when I need to re-focus, I imagine that I'm in this Mountain Pose. I feel my feet firmly on the floor, connect with my power center, and move on.

Lastly, let's say you are feeling scared or agitated or just need a calming influence and want to create a visualization that will help you to feel more peaceful. You have very specific elements in your visualization that you can regulate to help you achieve these results. You can always make your images more or less vivid by increasing or decreasing the intensity of the surrounding colors or the lighting in the space. You can even change how your senses are engaging with the space. For example, I love the beach and the sound of the ocean. I can imagine that I'm at the beach. I can pick the time of day, the location, and the intensity of the sun. I can have my feet in the water or I can look at the ocean from a distance. I can make the water dark blue like the Mediterranean or light green like the Caribbean.

You get the idea. Have fun with these visualizations. You are only limited by your imagination. The more you practice sensing, feeling, and seeing the more powerful your visualizations will become.

CHAPTER 16
Putting It All Together

Congratulations!

I know the kind of commitment and courage it takes to take a good, hard look at yourself and to be willing to go through the process of change. I call this the work of the warrior. You are a warrior!

Let's review what you've accomplished. In Chapter 4, we looked at increasing your ability to focus. We talked about the bursting field of neuroscience and the process of neuroplasticity—which is all about creating new pathways in the brain. Remember the phrase "neurons that fire together, wire together." Over the time you have been working through this book, through the practices of focusing, meditation, and mindfulness, you have been creating new awareness, new habits, new behaviors, and, therefore, new neural pathways. You have learned about the sympathetic and parasympathetic nervous systems and how to initiate a relaxation response through three-part breathing or yogic breathing.

Chapters 4, 5 and 6 were focused on calming down the body. Then, we moved onto managing and changing your thoughts; beginning with mindfulness training, which gave you mechanisms to observe your bodily sensations and your thoughts without judgment, which, again, helped you to raise your level of awareness.

From mindfulness we looked at your belief systems: those underlying thought patterns that rule your behavior. Remember that when left unconscious and unexamined, belief systems have tremendous power over you. Having taken the time to investigate these belief systems, however, and consciously choosing those beliefs and values that serve you in your current life, you became the master of your own universe—rather than being battered around by thoughts and feelings that kept you swirling.

Once you had some awareness of those belief systems or thought patterns, we looked at changing those thoughts that were negative and transformed them into what I call "productive" thinking—always asking the question, "Do my thoughts produce something useful for me or do they take me down that negative spiral?"

We also stressed the idea that we create our own reality. It's always easier to blame someone else for our experiences. But, if you take responsibility for where you are in life, you also are empowered to change your condition—that's what empowerment is all about.

Then, we moved on to the topic of fear. There are those fears that are easy to recognize and appropriate like driving on an icy road. There are also subtle fears. We call these primary fears and they show up as themes or stories you told yourself when you were a child to explain things that you couldn't explain. Primary fears usually start with "I'm not _____ enough."

Then we went on to learn how to clear these fears so that you could make room for the positive feelings you want to bring in. You were given several powerful exercises to accomplish this clearing and replacing.

Lastly, we looked at creating powerful visualizations. You were given some ideas as to how you could use visualizations to your advantage and then how to create them for yourself.

Now we have come full circle. The skills you learned here need to be practiced and repeated. The training in this book is just the beginning of a life-long journey of self-responsibility and introspection. The more you use these tools, the more automatic they will become. In the beginning, practicing these skills is just like learning to ride a bicycle or driving a car. At some point, the information becomes embedded in your subconscious mind and you no longer need to think about all the strategies. You are now programming yourself to respond rather than react. How powerful is that?

If you have any questions or want to continue this journey with me, just get in touch. Email me at **tina@tinagreenbaum.com**. You can also visit my website **www.tinagreenbaum.com** and you can find my online Assessment Quiz at **www.masteryunderpressure.net**. I also speak internationally.

Congratulations, again, on a job well done!